CHURCH MUSIC SOCIETY PUBLICATION: 023A
Hon. General Editor: Richard Lyne

T0033734

for the Choir and Congregation of St. Mary's Church, Nor[t]

Saint Mary's Mass

Music by ANTHONY CÆSAR

Kyrie

Alternative version of Kyrie

Gloria

Allegretto giocoso

Glo-ry to God in the high-est, and peace to his peo-ple on earth. — Lord God, hea-ven-ly King, al- -migh-ty God — and Fa - ther, we wor-ship you, we give — you thanks, we praise — you — for your glo - ry. Lord — Je-sus Christ, on-ly Son of the Fa - ther, Lord God, Lamb of God, you take a-way the sin — of the world: have mer - cy on us: you are seat-ed at the right hand of the Fa - ther: re - ceive — our prayer.

Tempo primo

For you— a-lone are the Ho-ly One, you a-lone are the Lord,—

cresc. *f*
you a-lone are the Most High, Je-sus Christ, with the Ho-ly Spi-rit,

allargando *ff*
in the glo-ry of God— the Fa-ther. A — men. A — men.

Gospel Responses

mf
Glo-ry to Christ— our Sa - viour.

mf *f*
Praise — to Christ — our Lord. —

Sanctus – Benedictus

Andante solenne *pp*
Ho - ly, Ho - ly, Ho - ly Lord, God— of pow'r and

più mosso *mf* *f*
might, heav'n — and earth are full— of your glo - ry. Ho-san-na in the

mf
high-est. Bless - ed is he who comes— in the name— of the

f *ff*
Lord. Ho-san-na in the high-est, Ho - san-na in the high - est.

Acclamations

Agnus Dei

Acknowledgment

The *Gloria*, the *Sanctus*, the *Benedictus* and the *Agnus Dei* from *The Order for Holy Communion Rite A* from the Alternative Service Book 1980 are © International Consultation on English Texts and are reproduced with permission of the Central Board of Finance of the Church of England.

Origination by Jeanne Fisher, Ludlow, Shropshire
Printed by Halstan & Co. Ltd., Amersham, Bucks

Pack of 10 copies
Not available separately

ISBN 0-19-395363-3

9 780193 953635